3 1833 00769 004

P9-EDT-117

Washington's America

Washington's America

BY ROBIN McKOWN

EXITUS ACTA PROBAT

George Washington

J B
W 277 mck

PUBLISHERS Grosset & Dunlap NEW YORK

© ROBIN MCKOWN 1961

ALL RIGHTS RESERVED

To

CAPTAIN BURKE

MANUFACTURED IN THE UNITED STATES OF AMERICA

Foreword

1422630

Washington's Statue at the World's Fair

George Washington was a product of his times, of the society in which he lived, and of the epoch-making events that shook this country between his birth in 1732 and his death in 1799.

Within that period, thirteen American colonies, all children of England, grew from infancy to adulthood. They quarreled among themselves in brotherly fashion, began to expand westward and to develop their own industries. They stormed at the apron strings that bound them to the mother country, rebelled, united with each other, and won a war for independence. Then they came to realize the need for a strong central government. They adopted a Constitution and launched the first massive experiment of a democratic government.

The man who led the colonies in war and in peace grew as they did. He shared their sufferings, their struggles, their restlessness, their triumphs. He learned by mistakes as they learned. He was a man of iron will, capable of anger, enthusiasm, discouragement, bitterness, and faith in the accomplishment of the impossible. He possessed generosity, patriotism, charity, a love for property and possessions, sternness, self-pity, modesty, pride and a host of other contradictory passions. He be-

came a great man as the colonies became a great country.

There was no one else like him, yet the qualities that were part and parcel of his nature are in all Americans.

No man's name is better known than that of the first President of the United States. The nation's capital is called after him, as are twenty-six other United States towns and villages, thirty-two counties, one state, and eight colleges and universities. There is a Lake Washington, Cape Washington, Fort Washington, Mount Washington, Washington Harbor, Washington Heights, Washington Crossing. There are Washington Parks and Washington Squares by the dozen. We see his portrait on coins and banknotes and postage stamps. His birthday is a national holiday.

Unfortunately, the homage paid to George Washington, Father of Our Country, has clouded almost completely George Washington, the man. Generations of well-meaning biographers have recited legends of his childhood to prove that, unlike other little boys, he never did a naughty thing. Facts have been twisted into fiction to make of him a plaster saint. The real Washington has been submerged beneath this tangled growth of fantasy and fable. For most, he is a stranger, a man who has remained an enigma for over two hundred years.

What was he really like — this man with the immortal name?

Contents

ACKNOWLEDGMENT

For their courtesy and cooperation in supplying the pictures in this book the author gives grateful acknowledgment to the following:

CULVER PICTURES, INC.

CHARLES PHELPS CUSHING

FEDERAL HALL MEMORIAL ASSOCIATES

FORT NECESSITY NATIONAL BATTLEFIELD

GEORGE WASHINGTON BIRTHPLACE NATIONAL MONUMENT

INDEPENDENCE NATIONAL HISTORICAL PARK

LIBRARY OF CONGRESS

MOUNT VERNON LADIES' ASSOCIATION

NEW YORK PUBLIC LIBRARY

SERVICES CULTURELS AMBASSADE DE FRANCE

VIRGINIA DEPARTMENT OF CONSERVATION AND ECONOMIC DEVELOPMENT

West Front of Mount Vernon, engraving published in 1840 (2). George Washington, Gilbert Stuart painting (6). Washington's Statue at the World's Fair (9). Bridges Creek (14). George and His Father, painting by G. G. White (16). Wakefield Farm, A National Monument reconstruction (18). George Washington Drilling His Schoolmates (19). Lawrence Washington (20). Mary Ball Washington, attributed to John Wollaston (21). Young George and His Mother, painting by Alonzo Chappell (22). Washington as a Surveyor (24). Survey of Bridges Creek Area Made by Washington at Age 15 (24). Washington and George Fairfax, old engraving (25). Mount Vernon, old engraving (26). George Washington as a Colonial Soldier, painting by Charles Willson Peale owned by Washington and Lee University. The original hangs in the Lee Chapel, Lexington, Va. (28). Burning of Deerfield, Mass., old engraving (29). Washington and Christopher Gist, 1857 engraving from a painting by Alonzo Chappell (30). Washington and Indian Guides going down the Ohio, old engraving (31). Washington and Gist on a raft, old engraving (32). Washington Falls in the River, old engraving (33). Braddock's March, 1755 engraving from a picture by A. B. Frost (34). Death of Braddock, old engraving from a Chappell painting (36). Fort Necessity, a reconstruction (37). Plan of Fort Necessity (37). Washington Hoists the British Flag over Fort Duquesne (38). Arrival of the Indians at the French Camp (39). Washington and the People of Winchester (40). Washington's First Visit to Martha Custis (42). West Front of Mount Vernon, 1858 engraving (43). Marriage of George Washington and Martha Custis, painting by J. B. Stearns (44). Washington and His Family at Mount Vernon, engraving by Thomas Philibrown from a painting by Alonzo Chappell (46). Mount Vernon Pantry (48). Washington's Desk (48). Washington's Bedroom (49). George Washington at Mount Vernon (50). A Continental Soldier, engraving by J. P. McRae from a picture by Alonzo Chappell (52). A Ball in Old Virginia, engraving (53). Patrick Henry Addressing the Virginia House of Burgesses, H. B. Hall engraving from a painting by Chappell (54). The Stamp Act (55). The Boston Massacre, old engraving from Chappell painting (56). The Boston Tea Party, old engraving (58). Paul Revere's Ride, old engraving (58). The Signal in North Church, old engraving (58). Retreat from Concord, engraving by James Smillie from a painting by Chappell (59). Minutemen at Concord Bridge, a drawing by Alonzo Chappell made over 100 years ago (60). Washington at Princeton, painting by John Trumbull (62). The Washington Elm (63). Washington Takes Command at Cambridge, old engraving (64). Thomas Jefferson, engraving by Dequevauvillier from a drawing by Le Baron Desnoyers (65). Declaration of Independence, facsimile (65). Thomas Paine, old engraving (65). Common Sense, facsimile (65). Washington at Brooklyn Heights, 1860 engraving (66). Surrender at Trenton, engraving from a Chappell picture (68). Washington Crossing the Delaware, engraving from a painting by Emanuel Leutze (69). Surrender of General Burgoyne, engraving from a painting by John Trumbull (70). Alexander Hamilton, engraving from a Chappell picture (71). Valley Forge, magazine drawing (71). Lafayette, old engraving (72). Washington Rebukes Charles Lee, magazine drawing (73). Surrender at Yorktown, old engraving (74). The First Cabinet, painting by Alonzo Chappell (76). President Washington's Carriage, old engraving (77). The Constitutional Convention (78). The First Inauguration, engraving from the painting by John Froelich (80). Crowds Cheer at the Inauguration, old painting (81). Washington and Hamilton, engraved by Thomas Philibrown from a Chappell painting (82). The Cotton Gin, magazine illustration (83). John Fitch's First Steamboat, picture by Reigart (83). Martha Washington's Reception, old painting (84). The First Presidential Mansion, old engraving (85). Washington at Mount Vernon in 1797, Currier lithograph (86). Mount Vernon, Currier & Ives engraving (88). Martha Washington and George Washington, old engravings (89). The Washingtons and Their Grandchildren, painting by E. Savage (90). Death of George Washington, engraving by H. S. Sadd from the T. H. Matteson painting (92). The Battle of Breed's Hill, 1842 engraving by J. N. Cimbrede from the painting by John Trumbull (94).

Washington's America

I. A Boy Grows Up in Old Virginia

On February 11, 1732, at 10 o'clock in the morning, a boy was born to Mary Ball Washington and her husband, Augustine Washington, a Virginia planter. It was their first child and they named him George, after a friend. The date and the time of his birth were noted in the family Bible. Some twenty years later, when the Gregorian calendar was adopted, George Washington's birthday was officially changed to February 22nd.

His birthplace in Virginia's Westmoreland County was called Wakefield Farm. It was built on a small rising, and to the east and northeast Popes Creek flowed around it on the way to the Potomac. To the north was a lush spot known as Dancing Marsh, beyond which Bridges Creek also headed to the Potomac.

The farm has long since burned down, but the foundations show that it was solidly made, at least partially of brick. It must have been spacious. An inventory of its furnishings included ten bedsteads, thirteen tables, fifty-seven chairs, and accessories for eight fireplaces. The finest quality silver, pewter, and glassware, all imported from England, graced the table.

George Washington's father was a man of property and social standing — part-owner of two iron furnaces, proprietor of land and buildings in three Virginia counties, master of at least forty-nine slaves. The world which George first saw was one in which misery had never set foot. Inside were all the comforts of a well-run Colonial mansion; outside, the blue sky, the green sun-drenched farmlands, the ever-present cadence of rippling waters.

What a remarkable child! Like all mothers, Mrs. Washington surely said this many times, as she watched her small son learn to crawl, to toddle, to walk, to speak his first words. Like all mothers, she must have felt there had never been a child as clever and talented as hers. But unlike American mothers of a later date, she did not dream that he might one day become President of the United States.

There was then no United States of America — only thirteen colonies strung along the eastern coast of a vast continent. The colonies had their own legislatures and courts of law but were still under the rule of England. Eight of them, including New York and Virginia, had Royal Governors appointed by the British Crown.

In contrast to industrialized England, farming and fishing were the main occupations of the colonists. Great Britain looked to the colonies for raw materials but expected them in return to buy manufactured goods. They could make straw hats in their own homes, but manufacturing cloth or

Bridges Creek near Wakefield Farm where George Washington was born

felt hats was forbidden. While there were no textile mills, the wives and daughters of the colonists dressed flax and carded wool at home and wove cloth on a cumbersome hand loom. Blacksmiths, shoemakers, soap and candle makers supplied local needs, but most household and farm articles had to be imported from the mother country.

America had its rich and its poor, its slaves and its free men, but in comparison with England, the distinctions were mild. In England, the starving poor were herded in crowded and filthy slums, or rotted in debtors' prisons. A boy of ten was hanged for stealing a penknife; a fourteen-year-old girl was condemned to the same fate for taking a handkerchief. The rich yielded to every extravagant whim: a duchess lost a million pounds at cards in one night. In America there was employment for any able-bodied man or woman. The well-to-do often worked side by side with their servants.

The colonists were of many nationalities, Dutch, Swedish, German, Scotch-Irish. Some had fled from religious persecution. Others had come simply to escape the wars and wretched living conditions in Europe. The majority were of English descent, followed English customs, and believed it to be their moral duty to uphold the sacred rights of the British Crown.

"Most Gracious Sovereign," the colonists loyally called their faraway king even up to the eve of the Declaration of Independence. But it was not so easy to give allegiance to the King's representatives, who all too often proved lacking in kingly qualities. When George Washington was three, a German-born printer named Peter Zenger lay in prison for daring to publish a newspaper criticizing New York's Governor Cosby, a greedy man whose past was clouded with shady dealings. In a trial by jury Zenger was acquitted, a historic event which established the principle of the freedom of the press.

In that same year the Washington family moved

[17]

The legend of George Washington and the cherry tree has become part of American tradition

to George's second home, up the Potomac to Hunting Creek lands, where Mount Vernon now stands. George was not yet seven when they moved again, this time to Ferry Farm, on the Rappahannock River, across from picturesque Fredericksburg. Here, according to legend, young George once tossed a Spanish dollar across the river "to see how far he could make a dollar go." Tourists have tried to do the same but have found the feat impossible.

Many fanciful tales are told about him as a boy, the most popular being that he once cut down a cherry tree and afterwards confessed to his father, saying, "I cannot tell a lie." Parson Mason Locke Weems, in whose biography of Washington this story first appeared, actually never credited six-year-old George with cutting down a cherry tree,

only with cutting through the bark. True or not, the cherry tree story lives on as part of American folklore.

By the time the Washington family moved to Ferry Farm, George had five younger brothers and sisters, Samuel, Jack, Charles, Betty, and Mildred. In 1743, Augustine Washington died unexpectedly. He left all his children well provided for. To George went Ferry Farm and other property including ten slaves, to be kept in his mother's charge until he was twenty-one. Did he, at the age of eleven, help care for the little ones or share the duties of the farm? Again, this is a question no one can answer with certainty.

Two other members of his family assumed importance to him about this time. These were his older half-brothers, Lawrence and Austin, sons of

his father by an earlier marriage. During most of his early childhood they were away attending school in England. Lawrence was fourteen years older than George, Austin, thirteen years older. Lawrence followed his English education with a stretch as a Colonial officer under the British Admiral Edward Vernon in the campaign against the Spanish in the Caribbean port of Cartagena.

The war was the climax of a long simmering dispute between England and Spain over maritime rights in the West Indies. It had flared up when a merchant captain named Jenkins claimed that Spanish privateers had boarded his vessel, tied him to a mast, and cut off his ear. Indignation at this outrage resulted in an expedition to capture Cartagena, which was a mere huddle of Spanish huts of no strategic value. Some three thousand American colonists volunteered to fight, Lawrence Washington among them.

Although the British troops were paid, clothed, and fed, there was no provision for the Americans. In the blistering sun they had to wear their own heavy homespun woolens. Hungry and miserable, they tramped through malaria-infested swamps, while gunfire poured down from hidden sources. The English and Americans were badly beaten. Only some eleven hundred of the colonists lived to return, nearly all, like Lawrence, suffering from malaria or the seeds of tuberculosis. Later it turned out that the sea captain Jenkins had lost his ear in a common brawl and had made up the story of the Spanish attack. Lawrence Washington's young brother knew nothing of the futility and horror of this campaign.

George admired both his half-brothers, but he worshipped Lawrence, the tall, tanned young man back from the wars. Austin inherited the Wakefield lands from their father and soon was settled there with his bride. To Lawrence went the Hunting Creek lands. Here, on his return from the West

Indies, he built a house of typical Virginia Colonial architecture. In honor of the Admiral under whom he had served, he named it Mount Vernon. Soon he married Ann Fairfax, the daughter of a neighbor. George visited his older brothers frequently, but Mount Vernon became his second home, and at fourteen he moved in with Lawrence and his wife.

By this time he had all the formal schooling he would ever receive, first from a tutor and then at a small local school. He had a bold and legible handwriting, excelled in mathematics, but was then and later a poor speller. He knew something of

George may have drilled his schoolmates in war strategies learned from his older brother, Lawrence

akefield Farm—A Reconstruction. Only the undations remain of George Washington's birthplace

Lawrence Washington. Young George adored his older half-brother,
who had studied in England and fought at Cartagena

social conduct too, and had copied down in a note-book 110 "rules of civility" from a widely read book called *Youth's Behavior*. They included such admonitions as:

> "Sleep not when others Speak, Sit not when others Stand, Speak not when you should hold your Peace, walk not when others Stop.
>
> "Superfluous Complements and all Affectation of Ceremony are to be avoided, yet where due they are not to be Neglected.
>
> "Let your recreations be Manfull not Sinfull.
>
> "Talk not with meat in your mouth."
>
> "Labour to keep alive in your breast that little Spark of Celestial Fire called Conscience."

Lawrence worried about the future of his young half-brother. In his position as captain in the British Navy, he found George a midshipman's berth, thinking that a life at sea might be to his taste. George's mother, learning of this plan, wrote for advice to her brother, Joseph Ball, in England. It would be a great mistake, he promptly wrote back. George would be better off apprenticed to a *tinker*, than to go to sea. His letter put an end to the matter once and for all.

George's disappointment did not last long. Mount Vernon offered many compensations, fishing, swimming, horseback riding, hunting. He became a superb horseman and an excellent shot. Sometimes Lawrence's comrades of battle came to visit and George listened avidly to tales of their wartime experiences. One of them, a Dutch soldier of fortune named Jacob van Braam, taught him fencing.

The glamorous Fairfax family into which Lawrence had married lived in a beautiful house at Belvoir, some eight miles away. Handsome George William Fairfax, brother of Lawrence's wife, Ann, became young George's best friend and companion for fox hunting and other sports. The family was

Mary Ball Washington, mother of America's first President

cultured, hospitable, and gay. There were always young people and parties. Occasionally, Thomas Fairfax, a distant cousin, came to stay with them.

Lord Fairfax had gone to Oxford, and belonged to London's high aristocracy. Moreover he was an intellectual, and had contributed to Mr. Addison's *Spectator*, London's foremost literary journal. It is said that he left England because he was jilted on his wedding day for a rival with a higher title. This crusty old bachelor was proprietor of an incredibly vast estate of over five million acres. (This land was confiscated during the Revolution since Lord Fairfax was a British subject.) He took a fancy to George, impressed by his athletic prowess, his modesty, and perhaps by the deference the youth paid him. This young man, he announced one day, should have the privilege of surveying his lands. He would pay him well for it.

George was a good draftsman, thorough and

accurate in his measurements. For practice he made excellent surveys of Lawrence's turnip field and of Bridges Creek at Wakefield. In a country with as much uncharted territory as America a surveyor would never lack work. At the time he liked the idea of making this his profession.

In March of 1748, when he was just sixteen, he and George William set out on a surveying trip for Lord Fairfax in the yet unsettled part of Virginia. Loaded down with tripod, theodolite, and other equipment, they broke across underbrush, trampled through woods of maple, walnut, hickory, and chestnut, climbed mountains, slept on straw in primitive huts or, more comfortably, outdoors by a fire. On one occasion they met a tribe of Indians who, far from being hostile, let them watch their native dances. The two boys were gone a month and two days.

By the time the trip was over, George had become a trained woodsman and pathfinder. He had learned much of the ways of the Indians, wore an Indian hunting shirt, and knew how to move soundlessly through the dark forests. In his wanderings, he met some of the hardy frontiersmen who would be his future soldiers.

With this experience back of him, George was granted a surveyor's commission from William and Mary College and at seventeen was appointed surveyor of Culpepper County. But surveying, like sailing the seas, was not to be his life's work.

Lawrence had not been well since he returned from the Cartagena campaign. To try the benefits of a change of air, George accompanied him to the Barbados, the most easterly island of the West Indies. This was George's first and only trip outside of America. It started out magnificently. He noted in his diary that he caught a dolphin, a shark, and a pilot fish all in one day. Then a hurricane came up, presaging trouble. In the Barbados, the brothers were warmly received and invited every-

[23]

Mrs. Washington convinces young George not to go to sea as a midshipman

*George Washington and George William Fairfax
survey Lord Fairfax's vast estate in Virginia*

*Survey of Bridges Creek area made by
George Washington at fifteen*

George Washington and George William Fairfax often went fox hunting together

where, but at one home where they dined there was a case of smallpox. Two weeks later George came down with that disease, which marked him with scars for the rest of his life.

Nor did the trip cure Lawrence's tuberculosis. He lived only a few months after his return to Mount Vernon. In his last days he formally resigned his position as one of Virginia's four adjutant-generals. George was appointed in his stead, given the rank of major and the sizable annual income of 150 pounds.

By the terms of his will, Lawrence left his Mount Vernon estate to his baby daughter, with the proviso that in case the child died, the estate should go to George except for an annuity to Lawrence's wife. The child did die shortly. Ann returned to Belvoir and her own family. Later she remarried. George paid her for her share of the estate in a lump sum.

By the terms of the will, he also inherited Lawrence's stock in the newly formed Ohio Land Company. The Governor of Virginia had granted this company some 500,000 acres of fertile land in the Ohio Valley, to be parceled out to enterpris-

Mount Vernon was bequeathed to young George Washington by his half-brother, Lawrence

ing settlers. Many years later, his Ohio Company stock would make George Washington one of the largest landowners in America. But first a series of battles had to be fought, a struggle known in history as the French and Indian Wars.

At twenty-one he was an exceptionally tall young man, lean and muscular, with pale complexion, reddish brown hair, steady blue-gray eyes. He was also Major Washington, sole proprietor of Mount Vernon and other lands. He bore the responsibility with dignity and with a certain sadness. His youth was behind him. He had lost his father in his childhood and the beloved brother who had been both father and hero to him. He had lived away from his mother's rule for years. He had gone into the wilderness, earned his own way, proved himself a man.

II. The Colonies Fight for the King

On October 31st, 1753, when George Washington had held his post as adjutant only a few months, Robert Dinwiddie, the burly Scottish Governor of Virginia, asked him to come to the Royal Palace of Williamsburg. He wanted him to deliver a letter and bring back a reply.

The task was not as simple as it sounded. The letter was to be taken to the French commander somewhere beyond the Allegheny Mountains. The French already held Canada and the St. Lawrence Valley on the north, and New Orleans and the Louisiana territory in the south. Now they were building forts along the Ohio, claiming all the western lands as their own. That they should dare think they could bottle up English subjects in a narrow strip along the Atlantic coast was considered an insult to the Crown. The letter Dinwiddie wanted young Major Washington to carry was a demand to the French to get out of the Ohio Valley. One Virginian had already tried to take the message but had given up, defeated by Indian harassment and the baffling country.

Since it was a volunteer assignment, Washington could have refused on the grounds that the management of Mount Vernon required his attention. It didn't occur to him to do so. Adventure and a chance to show his abilities — the offer gave him both. He started out that very day.

He was at Fredericksburg the next morning, where he enlisted the services of his brother's old friend, the Dutchman, Jacob van Braam. Van Braam spoke English poorly but he knew French, which Washington did not. They went on to Winchester, where they purchased horses and supplies, and from there continued to Wills Creek (now Cumberland, Maryland), the last English outpost.

A raid on Deerfield, Massachusetts, during the French and Indian Wars

George Washington as a Colonial soldier

[29]

Here Washington persuaded a rugged frontiers-man named Christopher Gist to act as guide, and engaged others to join their party, including two Indian traders.

It was already November 14th, and from the beginning heavy rains and snows held back their progress. With difficulty they reached the forks of the Ohio (now Pittsburgh) and proceeded seventeen miles down the river to the Indian village of Logstown.

"Brothers, I have called you together in Council by order of your Brother, the Governor of Virginia," Washington began his address to the tribesmen through his interpreter. His sincerity impressed them and he won, temporarily, their support against the "French Indians who have taken up the hatchet against us." A friendly Seneca chief known as Half King agreed to accompany them with a few of his men, Jeskakake, White Thunder, and the Hunter. Mires and swamps im-

Washington and Indian guides descending the Ohio. The last part of the journey to Fort LeBoeuf was made by canoe

[31]

Washington and Christopher Gist en route for Fort LeBoeuf

The return journey — Washington and Gist try to cross the Allegheny on a raft

peded their progress. The last lap of their journey they made by canoe, leaving their horses behind.

They reached their destination, the French Fort LeBoeuf (now Watertown, Pa.), on December 12th, almost a month after leaving Wills Creek. The elderly French commander, Legardeur de St. Pierre, received the party with the greatest courtesy, wined and dined them, and presented them with provisions for their return journey. But the answer he gave to Governor Dinwiddie's letter was "No." The French would not evacuate their forts. This country belonged to France, St. Pierre declared, by the right of LaSalle's early explorations.

Before they left, Half King came to report that the French commander had made him promises of love and friendship, and as a proof that he wanted to live with his Indian brothers, had offered to send supplies to the Indians at Logstown. The commander had also sworn to Half King that the country belonged to the French, that no Englishman had the right to be there.

"I can say that never in my Life I suffered so much Anxiety as I did in this Affair," Washington confessed in his journal.

But neither the French commander's fair promises nor his more obvious attempt to hold Half King and his men by the "Power of Liquor" succeeded. The Indian guides remained loyal to the tall American colonial who had engaged them.

The hardships Washington and his companions had undergone paled before those of the trip home. Winter had descended in full force. The horses were so weak and feeble that Washington left them and the baggage with Van Braam. In Indian garb, far more practical than uniforms, Washington and Gist proceeded on foot.

They had just passed an outpost with the ominous name of Murdering Town when a group of French Indians caught up with them. One fired at Washington at a distance of only fifteen paces but missed. From then on, it is said, the Indians believed George Washington led a charmed life.

When they reached the Allegheny they found the river jammed with blocks of ice. With one small hatchet, it took them a day to make a raft. The pole Washington used to propel them across slipped, and he fell in the icy water, barely managing to drag himself back on the raft. They could reach neither shore and spent the night shivering on a small island. Gist had both fingers and toes frozen, but somehow Washington escaped this mishap. The next morning the ice was solid, and they walked to shore.

Washington reached Williamsburg the day before an important council meeting. Though the answer he brought from the French was negative, Governor Dinwiddie was delighted with the cour-

age and enterprise he had shown. He had been tactful with the Indians and had acquired valuable information about the country they now knew they must fight for. The Governor insisted that Washington have the rough notes he had made on the journey ready to be presented at the council meeting. All night the young major labored by candlelight on this literary task. The document was later published, and copies were sent overseas to be studied by the King and Parliament. At home and abroad his exploit was discussed.

Washington nearly loses his life when his pole slips and he is thrown into the icy water

He was made a lieutenant colonel, and on March 31st of 1754, Dinwiddie sent him with a detachment of Virginia militia to fortify the disputed territory. At Great Meadows, some fifty miles beyond Wills Creek, they were joined by Washington's friend, Half King, who told them that a force of French and Indians were marching toward them from Fort Duquesne. The story was verified by one of Half King's runners: the French were hiding on Chestnut Ridge, five miles westward.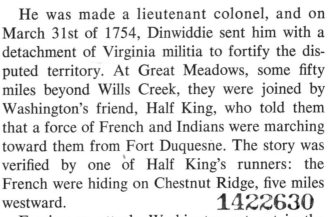

Fearing an attack, Washington set out in the dark of night with a party of forty soldiers and Indian guides. They found the French patrol camped in a glen. The French discovered their presence before Washington's men could encircle them. Shots rang out. The firing continued about fifteen minutes. When it was over, the French leader, Jumonville, and nine of his men had been killed. Washington had lost one man. The French and Indian Wars were officially launched.

Jubilant, Washington wrote to his brother, "I heard the bullets whistle, and, believe me, there is something charming in the sound." It was something only a very young warrior could have said.

While waiting at Great Meadows for reinforcements, he directed the building of small huts surrounded with trenches and a circular fort of upright logs. Fort Necessity, he named this primitive stockade. "That little thing upon the meadow," Half King called it contemptuously.

Fort Necessity was attacked in early July by a well-equipped force of some 700 French and Indians. Their leader, Captain de Villiers, was the brother of the slain Jumonville and intent on revenge. All day in a pouring rain, the enemy fired on the defenders of Fort Necessity, a scant 400 men of whom some 100 were ill. Washington no longer found the sound of whistling bullets charming. Thirty of his men were killed and seventy

[35]

General Braddock's splendid army starts out on the ill-fated campaign toward Fort Duquesne

wounded. Their cattle and horses were slain. At eight that evening de Villiers proposed a truce. Washington had no alternative but to surrender.

The terms, as Van Braam translated the sodden sheets by candlelight, seemed lenient. The French demanded their arms but no prisoners except for Van Braam and another, to be held for return of French prisoners. The next day the Americans journeyed sadly back to Wills Creek, the able-bodied carrying the sick and wounded. Because the surrender was an honorable one which saved the lives of many of his men, Washington was praised by the Governor and promoted to full colonel. But later he learned he had made a dreadful blunder.

The French terms referred to the *assassination* of Jumonville. Van Braam had translated this as the *death* of Jumonville. There was a world of difference. News of this slip reached Europe, where the young Colonial officer who had unwittingly admitted to murdering an enemy was held up to ridicule.

Although Dinwiddie and the British cleared him of any blame in the Jumonville affair, Washington was deeply mortified. In war, he had sought fame and glory. Instead he had been made the victim of a stupid error.

This was not his only cause for dissatisfaction. The British War Office had just ruled that Colonial officers, of no matter what rank, should be subordinate to officers holding a King's commission. Washington's resentment against British arrogance probably stemmed first from that ruling. He was outraged for himself and his fellow

Although George Washington won personal friends among the Indians, the majority gave their allegiance to the French

Fort Necessity — a Reconstruction. "That little thing upon the meadow," the Indian, Half King, called this primitive fort

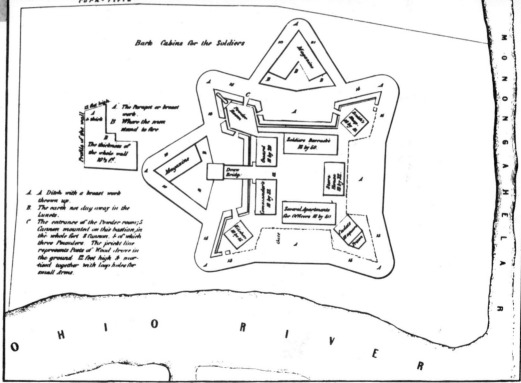

Plan of Fort Necessity

George Washington plants the British flag on Fort Duquesne which the French have deserted and left in flames

Colonials, resigned his commission, and in October of 1754 retired to Mount Vernon.

The good that was being said about him both in America and abroad far exceeded the criticism. Major General Edward Braddock, sent over from England to command a massive expedition against Fort Duquesne, invited him to come along as his personal aide-de-camp. As aide-de-camp, Washington would not have a command, but the matter of rank would be avoided.

Braddock was used to the European type of warfare, fought in the open. In vain, Washington and other Colonial officers recommended back-woods fighting, where the men scattered behind rocks and trees. Braddock considered such tactics beneath his dignity.

With fanfare and bands, the general led his briskly marching, scarlet-clad troops through the silent green forests. On July 9th, 1755, they were within seven miles of Fort Duquesne. Suddenly a blood-curdling shriek filled the air. Volleys of shots came from everywhere and nowhere. The British fired wildly, often shooting down their own. Braddock fell mortally wounded. In less than two hours, the forest was strewn with the dead. Washington, although he was weak from a fever, valiantly stayed to fight a rear-guard action. He was not wounded, but four bullets went through his coat, and two horses were shot under him.

Braddock died four days later, on the way back to Fort Cumberland. Washington read his funeral services. He had hoped to learn much from this seasoned veteran. He learned only that refusal to accept new ideas may be fatal. They buried Braddock in the middle of the road, and the men marched over his grave so that no trace

When the French and Indians attack seven miles from Fort Duquesne,
Braddock falls, mortally wounded, and is carried from the battlefield

Women, children, and old men of Winchester express their gratitude to George Washington

of it would be visible to hostile Indians who might claim his scalp.

For his coolness and courage in battle, he was made commander of Virginia's militia. With a few hundred soldiers he was assigned to protect border towns from Indian raids along a 350-mile stretch. His gallop across the country to the rescue of beleagured Winchester won him the gratitude of the townspeople. But he and his men couldn't be everywhere they were needed. He sent plea after plea to Dinwiddie for reinforcements and supplies. The Governor, wrapped up in his own affairs, did nothing.

Washington served in one more campaign in the French and Indian Wars. In the year 1758, he went with British Brigadier General Forbes in another expedition against Fort Duquesne. By the time they reached the fort which Braddock had failed to take, the French had abandoned their claims to the Ohio Valley and departed, leaving Duquesne in flames. Washington hoisted the British flag over the smouldering ruins.

He had given five years to this erratic war, and now he sent in his resignation. The fighting continued intermittently for another five years until, by the Treaty of Paris in 1763, France gave up all territory in North America except for Louisiana and the "island" of New Orleans. By then Washington's strenuous war experiences had receded to a memory, hardly credible in view of the new pattern of his life.

for protecting them from Indian raids

Washington's first visit to Martha Dandridge Custis, his future bride. With her are her two children by her first marriage, Martha Custis and John Parke Custis, whom Washington nicknamed Patsy and Jacky

III. Mount Vernon

George Washington was a man's man, at home in the saddle with his comrades of battle. Still he had not reached the age of twenty-six without thinking himself in love on several occasions. There had been Mary Cary, Lucy Grimes, and Mary Bland. There had been lovely Betsy Fauntleroy and the delightful New York belle, Mary Philipse. At various times he had composed poetry to these young women, and more than once he had proposed marriage.

Before he went to war, he had met with no success. The girls had treated him fondly but invariably turned him down, often to marry someone else. Perhaps his approach was too timid. They must have noticed he was unsure of himself, slow thinking, with no gift for the smart chatter of the drawing room.

He found Mount Vernon, empty, lonesome, and neglected on his return. Often he fled from it to visit the Fairfax family at Belvoir. George William was married now to a beautiful and fascinating lady named Sally. Husband and wife welcomed him home like one of the family. Their happiness together made his own bachelor existence seem all the more barren.

Mount Vernon needed a mistress, there was no doubt of that. The war had given him confidence. No longer did the young women treat him lightly.

The war hero could have his pick. He chose a young widow with two children who lived in Williamsburg. Her name was Martha Dandridge Custis. She was the daughter of a Virginia planter, Colonel John Dandridge. At seventeen she had married Daniel Parke Custis, a man of wealth many years older than herself. His death had left her very nearly the richest woman in Virginia.

Martha did not have the striking beauty nor the sparkling wit of Sally Fairfax, but she was attractive in her own way, small, plump, with dark hair and hazel eyes. What appealed even more to the lonely Washington was her friendly manner, the way she had of making him feel at home.

Entrance to Mount Vernon

The marriage of George Washington and Martha Custis

Almost from the first time he saw her, he felt she was someone who would make him an agreeable companion for life.

They were married in the cold January of 1759 The only definite information of their marriage is a description of Martha's wedding gown. It was of white quilted satin, over which a heavy white silk, interwoven with threads of silver, was looped back with ribbons richly brocaded in a leaf pattern. The bodice was of plain satin and delicate lace, finished in a low, square neck. Strings of pearls were woven in her hair. Her high-heeled slippers were also of white satin and had brilliant buckles.

George Washington's new wife owned a country home called the White House, on the York River, as well as a home in Williamsburg called Six Chimneys. They spent their honeymoon at the White House and then stayed on several months at Six Chimneys. The reason for the delay was that on his twenty-seventh birthday, he took office as a duly elected member of the House of Burgesses, the State Legislature of Virginia. As such, he automatically became one of Virginia's most distinguished citizens.

It was April when they set out by coach on the journey to Mount Vernon — George, Martha, Martha's children, two-year-old Patsy and four-year-old Jacky, servants, innumerable trunks, chests, boxes. Only then did it occur to George that he hadn't prepared a proper homecoming for his bride, a surprising oversight for one so thoughtful. To make amends, he scrawled a note to his manager, John Alton, and sent one of his servants ahead with it.

The key to the house was with Colonel Fairfax, he told Alton. He should get it, have the mansion thoroughly cleaned and make fires in the rooms of the first floor. He should also set up the bedsteads, see that the beds were made, get out chairs

and tables and have them well rubbed, and polish the staircase. He could inquire about the neighborhood for eggs and chickens and have them prepared in the best possible manner for the homecoming.

If Martha found Mount Vernon sparsely furnished compared with the luxury she had left, there is no record that she admitted it. The mansion, less impressive than it would be in later years, was charming as it was. The trees were in blossom, a purple haze shadowed the distant hills, and the view over the Potomac was magnificent. And there is every evidence that Martha was very much in love with the tall, serious man who had become her husband.

A new life began. Mount Vernon, which had stood empty and silent since Lawrence's death, now was filled with children's laughter and the bustling and chatter of cheerful Martha. Step by step, it took on the atmosphere of a gracious home.

In the beginning there were things to buy, endless things. They prepared long lists to be sent to England: a tester bed seven and a half feet long; blue and white canopy with bed cover and curtains to match; dessert glasses, Wilton carpets, firescreens and candlesticks, silver carving knives and forks with handles of stained ivory. Bibs, tuckers, and aprons (if fashionable) were ordered for "Miss Custis"; a black hair ribbon and silver shoe buckles for "Master Custis"; books for "children beginning to read"; ten shillings worth of toys. For himself, Washington ordered a book: "A New System of Agriculture, or a Speedy Way to Grow Rich."

His wife might be wealthy, but Mount Vernon must pay its own way. He was determined on that. He arose every morning at four, and after a breakfast of tea, hoe cakes and honey, set out on horseback for a tour of inspection. No matter

[47]

Washington and his family at Mount Vernon

was too minor for his attention. When a plow broke down, he repaired it himself. Often he took off his coat and mixed manure, killed hogs or pitched hay with the farm help. He discovered that tobacco, the mainstay of all Virginia planters, exhausted the soil, so he rotated it with Indian corn, potatoes, wheat, rye, winter barley.

In his daily inspection, he covered fifteen miles more or less. If there was too much snow for his horse, he went on foot. Unless he stopped for a fox or deer hunt, he came in for dinner at two or three. On the plantation he wore a plain blue coat, white waistcoat, black knee breeches, and boots. For dinner he invariably changed to a dark coat and white silk stockings, powdering his hair in the current fashion.

The farm work was mostly done by Negro slaves. At this time slaves were considered property. Later on Washington admitted that slavery was an unfair thing, though he never freed his own slaves. Where would they go and what would they do? As long as they were with him, he could see they were properly fed and clothed, and cared for when they were sick and old.

For skilled labor he often hired indentured workmen, men who sold their services for a period of years to pay back the price of their passage from Europe. Among them were millers, carpenters, shoemakers, masons, blacksmiths. With their wives and children they all came to live on the plantation.

Martha, not one of the idle rich, concerned her-

Mount Vernon pantry — on the small table at the home of the bride the Washingtons ate their wedding breakfast

The desk in George Washington's library where he kept his accounts and wrote in his journal

George Washington's bedroom at Mount Vernon

self with her children's tutoring, music and danc-ing lessons. Immaculately dressed in white, a ring of keys at her waist, she supervised all the work in the little houses that sprang up around the Great House — the weaving house, the dairy, the wash house, the smokehouse.

The kitchen was a separate building too. Here quarters of beef, rows of fowl, young suckling pigs were roasted on spits in an enormous fireplace. When the Washingtons gave a dinner party, a procession of servants with their platters and baskets moved hour after hour across the lawn from kitchen to dining room.

Hospitality was a rule and a code in old Vir-ginia. Relatives, friends, anyone with a proper in-troduction, could arrive unannounced, assured of food and lodging for themselves and their attend-ants, and fodder and care for their horses.

Such entertainment was reciprocal. The attrac-tive young couple were in demand at parties and balls at neighboring estates. There was an endless round of barbecues, fox hunts, races at Alexan-dria and Annapolis. Washington came to enjoy dancing and card playing, perhaps because in such pastimes there was no need to indulge in the trivial chit-chat at which, unlike his bubbling Martha, he never was any good.

Before his marriage he had been a lonely man, lonely and shy. Now all that was past. No longer did he watch George William and Sally Fairfax

Washington touring the plantation at Mount Vernon

with a pang of jealousy and discontent. With Martha at his side, he was secure with his companion for life. With little Patsy and Jacky to wave him good-by and to run up and greet him when he came home, he was a family man, with children he considered his own. With Mount Vernon, he was a patriarch, responsible for the welfare of a whole community.

In one of his orders to England, he had requested several busts of famous warriors: Alexander the Great, Julius Caesar, Charles XII of Sweden, Frederick the Great of Prussia. His London art dealer informed him there were none available. Instead he sent several Greek statuettes and two lions modeled after antique Roman ones "finished neat and bronzed with copper."

Washington accepted the substitution. Although he had asked for the warriors, he no longer wanted to model himself after them. What did he need of the glory of battle? He had everything he wanted where he was. But even in the first months of his marriage, events across the seas were forging his unique destiny.

The year 1760 brought George III to the British throne. He was a pale, uncertain youth just twenty-two, already showing traces of the insanity that would one day darken his mind completely. Never the tyrant he has been painted, his vacillating nature made him the victim of intriguing courtiers and a series of unscrupulous prime ministers, self-seeking men who saw the colonists not as a people struggling to make a better life in a new world, but only as a source of unlimited revenue.

George III was ruler of mighty England. George Washington was a private citizen of Virginia. The weakness of the first had already been proved. The strength of the other had not yet been tested. No two men could have differed more widely in temperament, mentality, and character than these two, around whom a great drama was in the making.

IV. The Making of a Revolution

As a member of the House of Burgesses, Washington came to Williamsburg every year, beginning with that of his marriage. When he was alone he rode horseback, but if he brought Martha and the children, they traveled in his fine coach with servants in white and scarlet livery. The journey took about ten days.

To visit Williamsburg was a real holiday. It was the most charming town in the South, with wide, tree-lined streets. Among its fine buildings were the Royal Governor's Palace, William and Mary College, and the Capitol, with the British flag flying high from its cupola, where the Burgesses had their meetings. There was also Raleigh's Tavern, where Washington often joined friends for a game of cards, perhaps in the Apollo Room with the Latin motto above the fireplace: "Hilarity is the offspring of wisdom and a good life."

As long as the Washington family was in Williamsburg, life was a series of gala social events. The women appeared in dazzling gowns of silk and satin imported, of course, from England. The men, too, were dressed in the height of English fashion, their hair carefully groomed and powdered. Outsiders would never have guessed that the seeds of revolt lurked even among these elegant couples dancing the minuet beneath the crystal chandeliers of a mirrored ballroom.

In spite of their air of prosperity, Virginia planters, Washington among them, were almost always in debt. They could sell their flour and tobacco only to England, usually in exchange for commodities. Transportation costs were heavy.

A ball in Williamsburg in Old Virginia

Continental Soldier

"If this be treason . . ." Patrick Henry addressing the Virginia House of Burgesses on the Stamp Act

The British hampered them in every move they made. Grievances against the Crown and Parliament were mounting, petty irritations and big ones.

Such matters were brought up at the House of Burgesses, but Washington, considering himself a poor speaker, took little part in the discussion. He was at this time more interested in enjoying himself, in improving Mount Vernon and increasing his land holdings than in politics. That vague term "personal affairs" kept him for some ten years from taking an active role in colony affairs. The change came gradually.

In the spring of 1765, Parliament passed a bill known as the Stamp Act, a direct tax on the colonies in the form of a stamp to be affixed to all legal documents, newspapers, books, marriage licenses, and even playing cards. A harmless measure, the English trustingly believed.

The House of Burgesses was nearing the close of its session when word of the Stamp Act reached pleasure-loving Williamsburg. A roughly clad young man of Scottish and Welsh descent

Anno Regni

GEORGII III.

REGIS

Magnæ Britanniæ, Franciæ, & Hiberniæ,

QUINTO.

At the Parliament begun and holden at *Weſtminſter,* the Nineteenth Day of *May, Anno 'Dom.* 1761, in the Firſt Year of the Reign of our Sovereign Lord *GEORGE* the Third, by the Grace of God, of *Great Britain, France,* and *Ireland,* King, Defender of the Faith, *&c.*

And from thence continued by ſeveral Prorogations to the Tenth Day of *January,* 1765, being the Fourth Seſſion of the Twelfth Parliament of *Great Britain.*

LONDON:

Printed by *Mark Baſkett,* Printer to the King's moſt Excellent Majeſty ; and by the Aſſigns of *Robert Baſkett.* 1765.

Anno quinto

eorgii III. Regis.

C A P. XII.

t for granting and applying certain Stamp ies, and other Duties, in the *Britiſh* Co- es and Plantations in *America,* towards her defraying the Expences of defending, ecting, and ſecuring the ſame ; and for nding ſuch Parts of the ſeveral Acts of iament relating to the Trade and Re- es of the ſaid Colonies and Plantations, irect the Manner of determining and re- ring the Penalties and Forfeitures there- entioned.

WHEREAS by an Act made in the laſt Seſſion of Parliament, ſeveral Duties were granted, continued, and appropriated, towards defraying the Expences of defending, protecting, and ſecuring, the Britiſh Colonies and Plantations in America : And whereas it is juſt and neceſſary, that Proviſion be made for raiſing a further Revenue within Your Majeſty's Dominions in America, towards defraying the ſaid Expences : We, Your Majeſty's moſt dutiful and loyal Subjects, the Commons of Great Britain in Parliament aſſembled,

4 A 2　　　　　　have

named Patrick Henry asked for the floor. Henry had a golden tongue and a heart of fire. He reeled off a set of resolutions that set the heads of the more conservative Burgesses whirling. He declared that any tax except that laid by the Virginia Assembly was "illegal, unconstitutional, and unjust." When someone murmured this was going too far, he shouted back his famous line: "Caesar had his Brutus, Charles I his Cromwell, and George III — may profit by their example."

Treason, some present suggested, but others agreed there was much in what young Henry said. His "Virginia Resolves" were printed and read throughout the colonies. By the time the stamps arrived from England, stamp distributors were burned in effigy, houses of royal officers were sacked, a new organization called the Sons of Liberty held parades of protest. The British were forced to repeal the hated Act.

Washington expressed his relief at the repeal in a letter to his English agent. If only England would let the colonies pursue trade and agriculture, he wrote wistfully, the "Mother Country" would profit in the end. Had this sensible advice been taken, a war might have been averted.

Instead Parliament passed the Townshend Acts, calling for duties on glass, lead, paper, paints, and teas. Even more insulting, the Acts gave government officials the right to search a man's property without a warrant and to deny the honored privilege of trial by jury.

George Washington, usually so imperturbable, flamed into anger. It seemed that the "lordly masters" of Great Britain would be satisfied only with "deprivations of American freedom." At the House of Burgesses he took the floor and proposed a "non-importation agreement," a retaliatory measure whereby the colonists would refuse to buy a long list of English goods, including hoes, axes, millinery, silks, calico, and boots.

[57]

The Boston Massacre, March 5th, 1770. British troops fired into a crowd who had been pelting them with snowballs; five were killed, six wounded

The Boston Tea Party, December 16th, 1773. Enraged by the tea tax, fifty citizens disguised as Mohawk Indians dumped 340 chests of tea into the ocean

Paul Revere, silversmith, craftsman, and patriot, spreads the alarm to Concord and Lexington and warns John Hancock and Samuel Adams

Old North Church in Boston. From its steeple, a lantern flashed the signal of the British advance. "One, if by land, and two, if by sea," were Revere's instructions

The other members listened to this tall Virginian with respect. His movements and gestures were graceful, his walk majestic. His silence was impressive. When he broke that silence, it was because he had something worth saying. Fond as he was of English luxuries, Washington took the lead in collecting signatures for the Virginia Non-Importation Association.

The British stationed several regiments in Boston, to help support their revenue laws. Independent Bostonians resented the intrusion bitterly. Making life miserable for the unfortunate British soldiers became a favorite sport. On March 5th, 1770, a group of these soldiers fired on some of their tormenters. Five were killed, and six were wounded. "The Boston Massacre," although admittedly the result of severe provocation, took its place in history.

Washington had personal matters to tend to in the next three years. He made a two-month tour through Ohio territory to inspect certain land claims there. He helped form a company to drain the Dismal Swamp in southeast Virginia. In his uniform he sat in 1772 for his first portrait known to be authentic, painted by a young Marylander named Charles Willson Peale. A year later, Washington's stepdaughter, lovely dark-haired Patsy, died at sixteen. The next year saw nineteen-year-old Jacky married to Nellie Calvert. The two youngsters settled down on a neighboring estate

At Concord Bridge, Massachusetts minutemen, aroused by Paul Revere, fired on British troops from Boston, launching the War of Independence

that Jacky had inherited from his real father. In one year Mount Vernon lost both the children who had brought it such joy.

During this time England, under pressure, rescinded all taxes except that on tea. It was a token tax only, since the British, from their East India Company surplus, were selling tea at half price. But the colonists would have none of it. In most big American ports, they seized the tea cargoes, stored them or sent them back to England. When the Governor of Massachusetts refused to let this happen in Boston, about fifty men, disguised as Mohawk Indians, boarded ships on Griffin's Wharf and emptied 340 chests of tea into the ocean.

The Boston Tea Party brought quick action from Parliament. The Port of Boston was ordered closed until the town paid for the ruined tea. General Thomas Gage, with whom Washington had fought in Braddock's campaign, was sent to occupy Boston with four regiments.

In Williamsburg, at a special session of the House of Burgesses, George Washington took the floor once more. "I will raise one thousand men, subsist them at my own expense," he said, "and march myself at their head for the relief of Boston." He had not been hasty in joining the rebellion. He had not been a leader, like Samuel Adams and John Adams of Boston. But once he made up his mind he offered everything he had—his money, his leadership, his reputation.

Retreat of the British. As the British fled from Concord back to Boston, farmers and townspeople joined the minutemen in harassing them

Although his offer was not accepted, he was made a delegate to the First Continental Congress, held in Philadelphia, in September of 1774. He went on horseback with two other delegates, the orator, Patrick Henry, and a Virginia businessman named Edmund Pendleton. At the Congress, held in Carpenters Hall, fifty-five delegates from all the colonies except Georgia adopted a "Declaration of Rights and Grievances." It demanded that Parliament repeal thirteen acts violating Colonial rights. One thing set Washington apart from the others. He wore his old Colonial uniform. More than words, it expressed his willingness to fight if it became necessary.

In the next months, while Gage held Boston in sullen submission, outlying Massachusetts towns began drilling their militia. "Minutemen" they called these soldiers who were ready to fight at a minute's notice. The midnight ride of Paul Revere, on April 18th, 1775, warned citizens of Lexington and Concord that British troops had ventured out of Boston and were headed their way. Minutemen at Lexington refused to disperse until the British fired. Though the British reached Concord and seized some cannon, their return journey was turned into a rout as shots rained down on them. Unofficially, the war for independence was under way. Rhode Island, New Hampshire, and Connecticut sent men to turn the Massachusetts army into a New England army.

The Second Continental Congress convened in Philadelphia at the State House, later known as Independence Hall, on May 10th, 1775. John Hancock of Massachusetts presided. George Washington was present — again in uniform. The Massachusetts Committee of Safety had sent an appeal begging the Congress to adopt the New England army as an American army and to set up a civil Colonial government.

Who should command such an army? John Adams proposed, "A gentleman whose skill as an officer, whose independent fortune, great talents, and universal character would command the respect of America and unite the full exertions of the colonies better than any other person alive. A gentleman from Virginia..."

At these words George Washington slipped unobtrusively into the library, perhaps from modesty, perhaps to wrestle with his conscience. He was aware that his nomination was due in part to the fact that he was a Southerner and might thus lead other southern colonies into the fray. He didn't want to fight. But even at that moment he knew he couldn't refuse.

The next day by unanimous vote he was chosen to be commander in chief. In his acceptance speech he said he appreciated the honor but was distressed, feeling that his abilities and military experience might not be equal to such an important trust. He added he wished no pay for his services. The only reward he could honestly accept was the realization that he was doing what he had to do.

He did not return to Mount Vernon. To Martha he sent a long and tender letter of farewell. On June 23rd, in the company of two of his newly appointed generals, he rode out to join his New England army. On the way they met a courier carrying a message to Congress. He told them that six days earlier the English had stormed Breed's Hill above Boston but that the New Englanders, under General Artemus Ward, had shot down wave after wave of the enemy, retreating only when the ammunition gave out.

This was the Battle of Breed's Hill, which, oddly enough, would go down in history as Bunker Hill. The men who had fought there would be part of George Washington's first command.

V. The Fight for Independence

Washington took command at Cambridge on July 3rd, 1775. He had expected some eighteen to twenty thousand men. He found some sixteen thousand, of whom only fourteen thousand were fit for duty. They occupied a ten-mile semicircular line of trenches from Charlestown Neck to Dorchester Heights. They were a motley collection of backwoodsmen, tradesmen, youthful adventure seekers, and grizzled farmers with seamed faces and gnarled hands. Most carried their own muskets, and few had uniforms. They lacked clothes, ammunition, food. They were lax in military discipline and strong in determination. He set up a plan of rigid training, strict obedience to officers, and harsh penalties for offenders. Some responded sullenly; others accepted his measures as a necessary evil.

General William Howe, who had replaced General Gage in Boston, was a few miles away. Without artillery and ammunition Washington could do nothing. In letter after letter, he begged the Continental Congress for funds and supplies. They sent committees to investigate but did little more. Congress could ask the colonies for support but could not enforce their demands. Early in the war they began printing money, but with only hope as security. The bills lost value fast, and "not worth a Continental dollar" became a maxim that would live.

The Washington Elm at Cambridge

While Washington fumed impatiently at inaction, a tragic scene was enacted in the north. General Richard Montgomery and Colonel Benedict Arnold, after harrowing journeys, met with their separate forces to wrest Quebec from the British. They were defeated. Montgomery was killed and Arnold severely wounded. Canada was lost forever to the colonies.

The month of March brought the artillery Washington had awaited nearly a year. The artillery had been captured at Fort Ticonderoga by Ethan Allen and the Green Mountain Boys of Vermont. The stout and capable Henry Knox, an ex-bookseller, had brought it to Cambridge by sled

Washington takes command of his army at Cambridge

and ox wagon through the roadless wilderness of upper New York.

Overnight heavy guns and cannons manned the crest of Dorchester Heights. General Howe in Boston stared through his spyglass in disbelief. He did not risk a fight but loaded his ships with men and supplies and sailed off. Washington's army marched back to Boston.

The word "independence," hardly mentioned at first, was in the air. This was due largely to a little book called *Common Sense* by Thomas Paine. Paine had come to America with a letter of introduction from Benjamin Franklin in England. He stayed to write and fight for America's freedom. *Common Sense,* a plea for that freedom, was read and discussed by colonists everywhere, working, as Washington said, "a powerful change in the minds of many men."

Six months after the publication of *Common Sense,* on July 4th, 1776, the Declaration of Independence, drafted by Thomas Jefferson, was adopted at a meeting of Congress in Independence Hall in Philadelphia. Washington read the thrilling document to his troops. But the word "independence" and the fact of it were still far apart.

General Howe had taken his fleet up to Halifax, where thousands of new troops joined his army, including German soldiers, paid to fight for England, whom the Americans called Hessians. With some 32,000 men and 500 vessels, he returned to New York and occupied Long Island. Washington had foreseen the move and was in Manhattan but with less than half the number of soldiers and no navy at all.

He had been criticized at Cambridge for doing nothing. Now he took action with disastrous re-

Thomas Jefferson, Washington's fellow Virginian, who drafted the Declaration of Independence

English-born Thomas Paine, author of COMMON SENSE, *which explained in words the common people could understand the reasons why America should be free*

[65]

Washington directs the evacuation of his men from Brooklyn Heights across the river to Manhattan

sults. He split his forces, sending about half to Brooklyn Heights. The British attacked on August 27th. Including prisoners, the Americans lost some 2000 men. Worse, they were in a trap. Any moment the British fleet, under Sir William's brother, Admiral "Black Dick" Howe, might close the escape route to New York. The American commander, who had only wanted to do his duty by his countrymen, was his own judge and jury for having led them to their death.

With the aid of John Glover's Marbleheaders from Rhode Island, Washington rounded up every boat available. In the dusk, his tall figure astride his great horse was everywhere, making sure his orders were carried out silently and quickly. By dawn his men were safe in Manhattan. He took one of the last boats. The British, aware at last of what had happened, swooped down too late. Their only capture was three soldiers who had stayed behind to plunder.

Washington's evacuation of Brooklyn Heights was a masterpiece of military strategy, but it was still a retreat. It marked the beginning of a dismal series of events. New York was abandoned to the Redcoats, while the Americans marched northward. Before they could move army and supplies to Harlem Heights, the enemy landed at Kip's Bay, scattering their militia like frightened animals.

"Are these the men I am to defend America with?" Washington cried, in shame and fury, and lashed his own officers across the shoulders. Then all alone he sat on his horse "like a dead man breathing" while an advance party of British drew to within a hundred yards. Death or capture — what did it matter now? One of his staff rode up, caught his bridle, led commander and horse out of danger.

It was his blackest moment. "If I were to wish the bitterest curse to an enemy on this side of the grave, I should put him in my stead with my feelings," he wrote sadly from Harlem Heights.

The retreat continued through New Jersey. Sometime in the course of it, Thomas Paine joined up, as volunteer aide-de-camp to General Nathanael Greene. At night by campfire Paine composed the first of a series of pamphlets which he named *Crisis*.

"These are the times that try men's souls," he wrote. "The summer soldier and the sunshine patriot will, in this crisis, shrink from the service of their country; but he that stands it *now* deserves the love and thanks of man and woman. Tyranny, like hell, is not easily conquered; yet we have this consolation with us, that the harder the conflict, the more glorious the triumph."

His words gave courage to the weary soldiers, as *Common Sense* had stirred the country. *Crisis* was published early in December of 1776. Several weeks later, on Christmas Day, Washington stopped retreating and attacked.

That night his ragged army filed through the snow down to the Delaware where Glover's Marbleheaders ferried them across the ice-clogged river. At dawn they reached the village of Trenton, held by Colonel Johann Rall and a contingent of Hessians. The Hessians had been celebrating the holiday the night before and were sleeping soundly. They woke to the sound of bullets. Nine hundred were taken prisoner that day. The Americans lost but four men. They pushed on to Princeton to defeat a second British force. News of these two fairly small victories spread cheer everywhere.

In the summer of 1777, the British sent a large force to Canada, headed by General John Burgoyne, to invade the colonies by way of Lake Champlain and the Adirondack Mountains. Howe, who had wintered comfortably in New York, was ordered to join him, the purpose being to pinch off the New England colonies. Instead Howe took his forces to Chesapeake Bay, some forty miles southwest of Philadelphia.

Washington was at his heels. In Philadelphia his soldiers paraded the streets with sprigs of green in their caps, some in brown work clothes or fringed Indian shirts, some in British or Hessian uniforms. Washington and his staff officers, astride their chargers, led the parade in uniforms of buff and blue.

At Washington's side was a red-haired, blue-eyed youth of twenty, a French volunteer, the Marquis de Lafayette. Lafayette had presented himself humbly to the Americans, begging to serve without pay in any capacity. He could speak little English. His interpreter was another young man whom the commander had made his aide-de-camp, Alexander Hamilton.

Their triumph was short-lived. An attempt to defend Philadelphia at the Battle of Brandywine failed, as did a counterattack at Germantown on October 4th, 1777. The British occupied the colonies' largest city. Congress fled to York, Pennsylvania. The blow was staggering.

When Washington's own prestige was at a low ebb, word came that on October 17th, General Horatio Gates had defeated Burgoyne's army of Redcoats at Saratoga. In truth, the victory was

Colonel Johann Rahl and his Hessian troops surrender to George Washington at the battle of Trenton

not surprising. Gates had 18,000 men. Burgoyne had been struggling helplessly through the wilds of the Adirondacks, ignored by Howe, deserted by his Indians. His force was reduced to some 5000 sick, hungry, homesick, and exhausted soldiers. Still Gates was credited with a splendid feat. In France, Burgoyne's surrender led Louis XVI of France to make an open military alliance with the Americans. The treaty binding the two countries was signed by Benjamin Franklin in Paris on February 6th, 1778.

In America, Gates became the man of the hour. Flattery went to his head. He began to think of himself as Washington's successor. In this ambition he was encouraged by an Irish volunteer named Thomas Conway, who, against Washing-ton's advice, had been made a brigadier-general. Back in York, Gates took up quarters at a public inn and gave lavish banquets, billed to Congress, for his supporters.

When the commander in chief learned of the Conway Cabal, as this conspiracy was known, the anguish of treachery was added to his other burdens.

Lafayette was invited to one of General Gates' dinner parties in York. Many toasts were drunk, but Washington's name was not mentioned. As the dinner came to an end, Lafayette rose and lifted his wine glass. "There is one toast which has not yet been drunk," he said. "Gentlemen, I give you General George Washington. May he remain at the head of the army until independence is won."

"The toast that saved the country," this tribute has been called.

That winter of 1777-78, Washington and his troops spent at Valley Forge, some twenty-two miles from Philadelphia. His men were in tatters. When trousers gave out, they wrapped themselves in blankets. Dirty rags replaced shoes. The sick, without proper medical care, suffered horribly. Their flimsy tents were small protection against the deadly cold; they split boards and felled trees to make a crude hut city. Only when this had been done did the commander move into Isaac Potts' stone house, which he made his headquarters. His life was cheered when Martha joined him there, as she did part of every winter of the war.

Another bright spot in those long months was the appearance of Baron von Steuben, a former Prussian military expert sent from France. From sunrise to sunset he drilled the men relentlessly, taught them military maneuvers while swearing at them in French and German. He was excellent for their morale. In the dreary plateaus of Valley Forge, a tough and disciplined army emerged.

General Howe fell in disgrace with Parliament because of his disobedience in the Burgoyne affair. He was replaced by General Sir Henry Clinton, who in June of 1778 moved the British army from Philadelphia to New York. Washington, with troops renewed by sunshine and more food, followed him, catching up with the British rear-guard at Monmouth, New Jersey, on June 27th.

On Christmas night, 1776, Washington crosses the Delaware for an attack on Trenton, held by the Hessians

General John Burgoyne surrenders to the American general, Horatio Gates, at Saratoga, New York, on October 17th, 177

He wanted Lafayette to lead an attack but had to yield when General Charles Lee claimed precedence as a senior officer. Lee, an ugly scarecrow of a man, was supposed to be an authority on the art of war. He was also a defeatist who believed that Americans could never stand up against trained British soldiers. Instead of advancing, he ordered a retreat. When Washington came up, he was aghast to find his men going in the wrong direction. He blasted Lee with a tongue lashing, sent him to the rear in disgrace, and urged the soldiers forward. "Never had I beheld so superb a man," Lafayette wrote of Washington's calm courage. The commander's quick action saved his troops from a rout, though because of Lee the British escaped serious casualties. By July they were once more in New York, while Washington's "skeleton of an army" camped at nearby White Plains.

In the South, Charleston had surrendered and Lord Charles Cornwallis was trying to subdue South Carolina. Congress sent Horatio Gates, the central figure of the Conway Cabal, to their relief. Gates failed miserably. So ignominious was his flight that Alexander Hamilton asked, "Was there ever an instance of a general running away, as Gates has done, from his whole army?" Congress humbly turned to Washington to name a successor. Washington, ignoring the rebuff of Gates' appointment, proposed General Nathanael Greene, a veteran of Trenton and Princeton.

Greene found "the shadow of an army in the midst of distress." Out of 2300 men, only about 800 were fit for duty. Their clothes were in tatters, their food supply down to three days' rations. All was not as hopeless as it looked. Among his Continentals were the tough Delawares and Marylanders, the self-reliant North Carolina and Georgia riflemen. Daniel Morgan, the "Old Waggoner," appeared to take over a command. Lieutenant Colonel Henry Lee, "Light Horse Harry," joined them and left with his legion of some 300 men to join Francis Marion, the "Swamp Fox," who was carrying on guerilla warfare in the South.

In a series of brilliant military tactics, Greene deployed his troops and edged Cornwallis and his sizable army into Virginia, where Lafayette, in charge of his first command, forced him on into the peninsula of Yorktown.

In July of 1780, Washington received a message that sent his heart pounding. It was from Newport, Rhode Island, and was signed by General Comte Donatien de Rochambeau. The French general had just landed in America with some 6000 first-rate, fully equipped regular soldiers. They were, he wrote, "under the orders of Your Excellency." Washington wrote back at once of the happiness with which he received "the auspicious news of your safe arrival."

Some weeks later, he conferred with Rochambeau at Hartford, Connecticut. On his return he stopped at West Point, the great fortress on the Hudson River, which he had recently put in charge of Benedict Arnold, the officer who had served so valiantly in the Canadian campaign. He knew Arnold was angry because of his lack of recognition from Congress, but was hardly prepared for what he learned at West Point. Arnold had fled

[71]

Alexander Hamilton, who became Washington's aide-de-camp

In the bitter cold of Valley Forge, campfires often scorched already worn out boots

to the British. In prison was a British officer, Major John André, captured in civilian clothes. In his shoes had been hidden detailed plans of West Point forts and other data in Benedict Arnold's handwriting. André was sentenced to death as a spy and hanged. He was said to have been a fop and a dandy, but he died bravely.

In the summer of 1781, Rochambeau's colorful French troops joined Washington's weather-beaten army on the Hudson. They built huts for the French officers, and French bakers erected enormous bread ovens. This was a ruse to make General Clinton think they were planning an attack on New York.

Instead they left bread ovens and huts deserted, while their two armies marched to Virginia to relieve Lafayette, who was besieging Lord Cornwallis and his troops in Yorktown. The success of their plan depended on the arrival of French Admiral Paul de Grasse, who was sailing up from the French West Indies with twenty-eight ships and a fleet of transports. When word reached them that de Grasse's fleet was safe in Chesapeake Bay, witnesses declared that Washington waved his hat in the air with joy.

They bombarded Yorktown for nine days. On October 17th, 1781, Cornwallis asked for a cease-fire. In the official surrender ceremony two days

General Washington blasts General Charles Lee at Monmouth for ordering his men to retreat instead of advance

The Marquis de Lafayette as a Continental Officer

The Surrender at Yorktown. General Benjamin Lincoln, acting for Washington, touches the sword of General Charles O'Hara of the British Guards, acting for Lord Cornwallis, in token acceptance of the surrender

later, General Charles O'Hara of the Guards led his Redcoats to the waiting French and American armies. Washington asked him where Lord Cornwallis was. Cornwallis was ill, O'Hara said, and had deputized him to make the surrender.

"A deputy should surrender to a deputy," Washington said gravely, and nominated General Benjamin Lincoln to act for him. Lincoln rode up, touched O'Hara's sword in token acceptance, then told the British Guardsmen where to stack their arms.

The surrender of Yorktown was the beginning of the end. The peace treaty was signed on September 3rd, 1783. Soon after, the British evacuated New York, and the American states were free.

"I have grown both blind and gray in your services," Washington told his men, as he took out his glasses to read them a final message.

At Fraunces Tavern, in New York, on December 4th, he met with his officers for the last time. Among those present were Baron von Steuben, Tadeusz Kosciuscko, a Polish volunteer, and Israel Putnam, whom Washington called affectionately "Old Put"; Horatio Gates, his erstwhile rival, Generals Henry Knox, Nathanael Greene, and Anthony Wayne. Silently they drank a glass of wine together.

"With a heart full of love and gratitude, I now take leave of you," Washington told them. "I most devoutly wish that your latter days may be as prosperous and happy as your former ones have been glorious and honorable."

Formally, he resigned his commission at Annapolis on December 23rd. The eight-year war had been fought on many fronts, and there had been many heroes. From it the commander in chief had emerged the best known and best loved person in the new United Colonies, the man whose integrity and fortitude had brought his country to victory. At long last, he was free to go home.

VI. A New Nation Is Born

Mount Vernon was a mirage of beauty after the death and desolation of the war. To Lafayette Washington wrote, "I am become a private citizen on the banks of the Potomac; and under the shadow of my own vine and my own fig tree..." At Mount Vernon, there were once more two small children to indulge and spoil and train. These were the son and daughter of Jacky, who had died in 1781 of tuberculosis, a baby, George Washington Parke Custis, and Eleanor, or "Nelly," a sprightly miss two years older than her brother. It was as though George and Martha were beginning life anew.

For just four years Washington enjoyed the pleasures of being a private citizen. All was not well in the country he had helped to free. Speculators were rich, while soldiers who had sacrificed everything were faced with ruin and starvation. A nation to be strong should have a strong economy. The Continental Congress had no power to regulate trade, make laws, or impose taxes. It could issue money but could not prevent the new States from printing money of their own in competition. The resulting chaos was inevitable.

In 1787, Washington was invited to Philadelphia as a delegate to a Convention set up to draft a Constitution, a sort of blueprint to guide the country in years to come. He was fifty-five and tormented by rheumatism. He tried to convince himself there were younger men to take over now. The "Celestial Fire Called Conscience" would not let him refuse.

The Constitutional Convention met at the State House, in the same room where the Declaration of Independence had been signed, on May 27th, 1787. The fifty-five delegates included young Alexander Hamilton and Benjamin Franklin, an old man of eighty. All the states were represented except Rhode Island. Through the sweltering summer, they met in secret sessions for endless hours of argument and discussion. Gradually these sessions evolved a document such as never before had been known.

President Washington's carriage. The carriage in which Washington rode to his Presidential inauguration

he First Cabinet of the United States. From left right, Knox, Jefferson, Hamilton, Randolph

George Washington presides at the Constitutional Convention of 1787 in Independence Hall, the State House, Philadelphia. Eighty-year-old Benjamin Franklin is seated, second from left in the front row

The Constitution provided for a Senate, composed of two members from each state, regardless of size, to be elected by state legislatures. There would be a House of Representatives, elected by the voters, on the basis of population. There would be a President, chosen every four years indirectly by electoral vote. A proposal from a South Caro-lina delegate that the President should be worth at least $100,000 was turned down. The question of slavery was by-passed. There was as yet no provision to change the ruling that a man must have property to vote. Giving women the right to vote was not considered. But provision was made so that the Constitution could be amended, as the

long years away from his "own vine and fig tree."

So limited was cash at Mount Vernon, he had to borrow to make the journey to New York. But from beginning to end it was a march of triumph. Everyone wanted to catch a glimpse of the tall, courtly man who had led them in war and who was now to lead them in peace. In Trenton, where he had defeated the Hessians, an arch twenty feet wide supported by columns twined with evergreen and covered with laurel was constructed. He was brought into New York on a barge rowed by thirteen ships' captains in white uniforms, escorted by dozens of other craft decked with flags and bunting. Flowers rained down on him in the parade to his new Presidential home at 3 Cherry Street.

April 30th, 1789 was Inauguration Day. George Washington rode to Federal Hall in his splendid cream-colored coach with his coat-of-arms emblazoned on its sides. The ceremony took place on the balcony. He stood stately and erect in an American-made brown worsted suit, his steel-hilted dress sword at his side, his hand on the Bible resting on a crimson cushion. Robert R. Livingston, Chancellor of the State of New York, administered the oath.

"Long live George Washington, President of the United States," Livingston cried. The cheers of the crowd below mingled with the roar of a thirteen-gun salute.

How should a President be addressed? His Majesty, the President? His Excellency, the President? Congress, not yet ready to discard titles of royalty, discussed the matter at length. Washington ignored the controversy and in the end he became simply Mr. President. Later that year, the twelfth colony, North Carolina, ratified the Constitution. Rhode Island held out until May, 1790. At last the thirteen colonies were one nation, indivisible.

Washington's mother died three months after

need arose. It went in effect the next year, as soon as nine states ratified it. By unanimous vote of the electors, George Washington was chosen as first President of the United States.

He accepted the honor with the feeling of a "culprit who is going to the place of his execution." It meant he would have not four but eight

Washington taking his inaugural oath. At the inauguration Washington wore a brown worsted suit of American make, as a symbol of America's new Independence

his inauguration. She had been living for many years with his married sister, Betty Lewis, at Fredericksburg, where he had seen her for the last time. The stalwart woman had become complaining and bitter in her old age. Washington had not been close to her since his childhood, but he had always treated her with generosity and respect, and the news of her death grieved him deeply.

He appointed Alexander Hamilton, his former aide-de-camp, as Secretary of the Treasury. General Henry Knox became head of the War Department and Edmund Randolph, Attorney General. As Secretary of State, Washington chose his fellow Virginian, Thomas Jefferson. Hamilton, Knox, Randolph, and Jefferson formed the country's first cabinet.

From the beginning there was dissension between Hamilton and Jefferson. Jefferson was concerned with the rights of the people. He believed strongly in free speech, free press, and free scientific inquiry. Hamilton held that the country should be ruled by those who owned the most property. "Your people is a great beast," he is reported to have said. Industrial inventions, such as John Fitch's steamboat and Eli Whitney's cotton gin, interested him more than pure science. He was for the development of more industry. Jefferson placed his hope in agriculture.

The President was the peacemaker between the two of them, but offered his support to many of Hamilton's daring measures, seeing rightly that they would lead to making the United States strong among nations.

The national debt must be paid, Hamilton said. The Federal Government should take over state debts as well. For this purpose revenue must be raised. In the eight years of George Washington's tenure, the energetic Secretary of the Treasury was responsible for a protective tariff on foreign goods, for the first United States Mint, for the first United States Bank, built in Philadelphia; for a long series of direct taxes on carriages, snuff, lands, houses, slaves, a stamp tax on legal documents unfortunately reminiscent of the one which had helped start the war, and a whiskey tax.

Taxes are never popular with those who have to pay them, but the whiskey tax was the one that caused the most furor. A good proportion of American whiskey was made by small farmers in their own stills. They didn't want anyone poking into their business. In 1794, some Pennsylvania farmers protested by burning the houses of tax collectors. The President quickly sent troops to suppress the Whiskey Rebellion. He proved that his government was indeed strong, but was severely criticized for calling out armed forces against the people.

Foreign policy also posed delicate problems. The French Revolution, begun gloriously on July 14th, 1789, with the storming of the Bastille, was inspired by the American one. France's Declaration of the Right of Man was a descendant of the American Declaration of Independence. But in 1793, the year that President Washington began his second term, Lafayette, the great friend of American freedom, fell in disgrace with the French Provisional Government and had to flee

[81]

Crowds cheering as Livingston cries out, "Long live George Washington, the President of the United States!"

the country. Later, he was arrested and put in prison in Austria. Louis XVI, whose timely aid had assured the victory of the colonies, was sent to the scaffold.

When war broke out between Great Britain and France, the French Republic reminded the American President that the Treaty of 1778 pledged mutual assistance in defensive wars. But Washington insisted the United States remain neutral. The country could not risk another war with England. His decision was unforgivable for those whose hearts were with France and her revolution.

The seat of Government moved to Philadelphia in 1790. The Presidential Mansion was the former Robert Morris house on Market Street, near Sixth Street. Here the First Lady of the Land gave her famous Friday receptions for the wives of those who held high official or social positions. Women were known to faint with joy on receiving an invitation from her. In the dining room of this mansion the President received visitors every

Tuesday afternoon at three. The guests were announced, one by one. As they entered they formed a circle, and Washington, beginning at the right, said a few words to each. The ceremony was over by four. More intimate visitors were invited to state dinners on Thursdays.

Gone were the days when Martha and George Washington could accept invitations from their friends at random, attend informal balls, suppers,

Eli Whitney's cotton gin revolutionized the cotton industry. It separated seeds from cotton at the rate of 300 pounds a day. By hand only five or six pounds a day could be cleaned

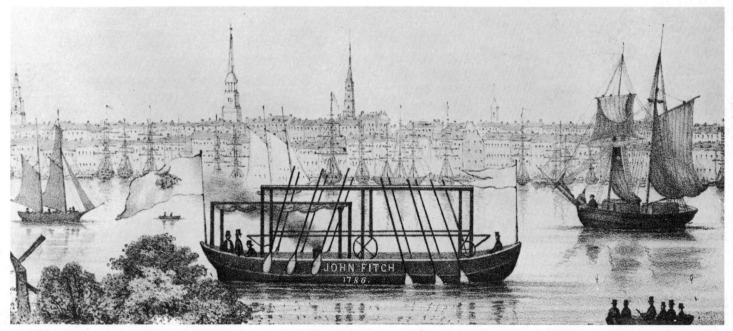

eorge Washington and Alexander Hamilton

To John Fitch, who died unrecognized, now goes credit for the invention of the American steamboat. His first was launched on the Delaware in 1787

One of Martha Washington's receptions at the Presidential Mansion

horse races. For the President, fox hunting and fishing were out of the question. The theater was almost his only relaxation. Once he went to see a comedy called *Poor Soldier*, in which he, as a Continental general, was described in comic verse. Everyone watched for his reaction. He burst out laughing. The next day all the newspapers mentioned that the President had laughed.

By the end of his administration three new states — Vermont, Kentucky, and Tennessee — had joined the Union. Turnpike roads were under construction. Coal deposits had been found in Pennsylvania. On the banks of the Potomac, Federal City, which would later be called Washington, D. C., was being laid out. A new country was under way.

In Washington's heart was the same feeling that had plagued him during his war service — that he had somehow not been equal to the trust placed in him. But the rousing cheers at the inauguration of John Adams were not for America's second President but for the man who was leaving public life forever.

The First Presidential Mansion, Pearl and Cherry Streets, New York City

Washington continued to make a daily tour of his plantation on horseback up until two days before his death

VII. The End and the Beginning

A young actor, strolling in the vicinity of Mount Vernon, stopped to help a man and woman who had been thrown from their carriage. He did not recognize the old horseman who galloped up to offer his assistance. When the overturned vehicle had been righted and the two men were dusting each other's coats, the stately stranger remarked that he had seen the actor in a play in Philadelphia. "But you are the President..." the young man gasped with sudden realization.

An overnight visitor, suffering from a heavy cold, lay coughing in his bed at Mount Vernon, unable to sleep. Unexpectedly he became aware of his host, in night attire, approaching his bed. The former President of the United States was bringing a bowl of tea, which he had made himself, to soothe his guest.

A fourteen-year-old girl named Harriet Washington sat down to compose a letter to her famous uncle. "I am a going to ask you My Dear Uncle to do something for me," she wrote. "...It will be for my good as all the young Ladies are a learning musick. I will be much obleiged to you if you will send me a gettar." A "gettar," she went on to explain, "is so simple an instrument that five or six lessons would be sufficient for anybody to learn."

Catherine the Great sent a request to the former President for a vocabulary of the languages of Ohio Indians. He prepared for her a word list of both the Shawnee and Delaware languages.

Mount Vernon, like its master, had reached its mellow years, showing the fruit of his intermittent labors. In some forty-five years the estate had grown from 2100 acres to 8000, divided into five farms — River Farm, Muddyhole Farm, Dogue Farm, Union Farm, and Mansion House Farm. Each was a complete unit with overseers, workers, livestock, equipment, and buildings. But it was at the Mansion House Farm, where Mount Vernon stood, that beauty took precedence over crop production.

For trees the proprietor of Mount Vernon had a special love. A visitor in 1798 mentioned peach and cherry trees, tulip trees, flowering magnolias, catalpas, dark green New Scotland spruce, weeping willows. The vineyard; the flower garden outlined by boxwood hedges; the kitchen garden with its vegetables, herbs, currants, raspberries, strawberries; the greenhouse holding plants from every part of the world — all were evidence of Washington's devotion to growing things.

The rectangular Colonial mansion which Lawrence Washington had constructed in George's

Mount Vernon. George Washington was his own architect for the colonnaded porch overlooking the Potomac

childhood was enlarged by two wings now, and a porch spaced with white columns stretched the full length of the house on the side facing the Potomac. Washington, so far as anyone knows, was his own architect. Improvements inside and out were all done by his masons and artisans un-der his detailed directions, often sent by letter when he was far away in space, if not in his heart. He and Martha, not an outside decorator, were responsible for the tasteful furnishings.

Lovely Mount Vernon had many visitors those two years from 1797 to 1799. One guest was made

welcome for months. This was George Washington Lafayette, the handsome eighteen-year-old son of the Marquis. The young man learned to like America and to master the American way of speech. Washington was fond of this youth as he had been of his father. On the wall of Mount Vernon's central hall hung a glass case with one of the President's most prized possessions, the Key to the Bastille, which his French comrade-in-arms had sent him.

Although he had retired to a life of "tranquil enjoyment," Washington had endless demands on his time, energies, and fortune. There never was a time when some of his many relatives didn't turn to him for advice or financial assistance. Every night after the rest of the family was asleep, he retired to his library, sat down at his desk, took out his quill pen, and by the light of two candles answered his voluminous correspondence, brought his accounts up to date, made entries in his journal.

Sculptors and painters from all over the world came to beg him to sit for them. When first he had his portrait painted he confessed he was as "restive as a colt is of the saddle," but later claimed that no drayhorse moved more readily "to his thills" than he to the painter's chair. No two artists painted George Washington alike, though all his portrayals have one thing in common — he is always grave and unsmiling. It is a pity for posterity that some artist could not have caught him waving his hat in the air with joy at the news that De Grasse's fleet was safe in Chesapeake Bay.

Though Martha and George were an old couple now, there was youthful gaiety in the house, as Nelly and George Washington Parke Custis grew into their teens. Nelly now played her harpsichord in the music room where little Patsy had practiced the spinet so many years before. Once as the young people were having a party, Washington stood at the doorway watching the dancing. The guests

[89]

George and Martha Washington, private citizens once more

Washington at home with Martha and her grandchildren, Eleanor Parke Custis and George Washington Parke Custis. Billy Lee, Washington's body servant, stands at right

caught sight of him and, awestruck, they froze into silence. He begged them not to interrupt their merriment and retreated.

His sixty-seventh birthday, February 22nd, 1799, was Nelly's wedding day. Her husband was Lawrence Lewis, son of Washington's sister, Betty. Nelly asked Washington to wear the grand embroidered uniform ordered for him in case there was a war with France. But the threat of war had vanished, and the fine uniform was never made. Instead he put on the worn buff and blue that had seen so many battles. She threw her arms around his neck and told him she loved him better in that.

As in his younger days he rose before dawn each morning and made the rounds of his plantation on horseback. "An old gentleman, riding alone, in plain dark clothes, a broad-brimmed white hat, a hickory switch in his hand, an umbrella with a long staff which is attached to his saddle-bow," he was described by one of the last of his friends to see him alive.

On Thursday morning, December 12th, he rode out as usual. A biting wind came up, carrying in its wake a mixture of snow and sleet. He didn't get back until three o'clock in the afternoon and, contrary to his invariable custom, he went in to dinner without changing his riding clothes.

The next day the heavy snow prevented him from riding, although in the afternoon he walked across the Mount Vernon lawns, marking some trees he intended to cut down. That night he complained he felt a cold coming on. About three he woke up in a fever, his throat so inflamed he could scarcely breathe, but he wouldn't let his wife get up in the cold to get help.

The next morning an overseer bled him, at his insistence, taking about a pint of blood. His secretary, Colonel Tobias Lear, grew alarmed at seeing him become weaker, and sent for medical aid. Three doctors arrived that day, first, Dr. Elisha

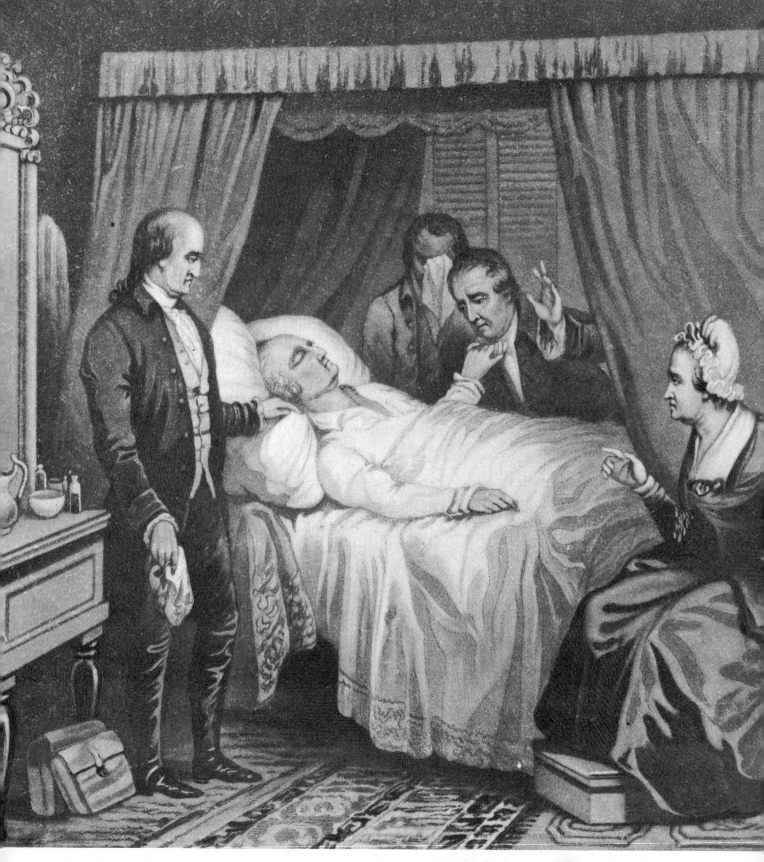

The death of Washington

Cullen Dick of Alexandria, and later Washington's regular physician, Dr. James Craik, and Dr. Gustavus Brown of Port Tobacco. Dr. Dick was opposed to another bleeding, which, in advance of his times, he thought a barbarous practice. The other two overruled him. More than a quart of blood was taken from the sick man that day.

Washington was in great pain toward evening. "I die hard, but I am not afraid to go," he told Dr. Craik. A little after ten his breathing became easier. He reached up and took his own pulse. Then his hand fell away.

"Is he gone?" asked Martha, standing at the foot of his bed. Told that he was, she said calmly, "I shall soon follow him." She outlived him just twenty-nine months.

It was 10:20 of the evening of December 14th, 1799.

George Washington, the man, was dead. George Washington, the Father of His Country, would live on forever as a symbol of the great nation he had helped to create.